the bad secret

to Janet,

with the beautiful
blonde hair —

Love

Judi '11

the bad secret
[POEMS]
Judith Harris

LOUISIANA STATE UNIVERSITY PRESS

BATON ROUGE

In memory of the mothers,

Dorothy, Jackie, and Barbara,

whose stillness is now a grace that will not startle the birds.

DESIGNER: Barbara Neely Bourgoyne
TYPEFACES: Democratica, display; Whitman, text
PRINTER AND BINDER: Edwards Brothers, Inc.

Library of Congress Cataloging-in-Publication Data
Harris, Judith, 1955–
    The bad secret : poems / Judith Harris.
      p. cm.
    ISBN 0-8071-3138-5 (alk. paper) — ISBN 0-8071-3139-3 (pbk. : alk. paper)
    I. Title.
PS3558.A6466B33 2006
811'.54—dc22
                                                                2005016504

The author wishes to express her gratitude to the editors of the following journals in which poems from this volume have previously appeared, occasionally under different titles: *English Journal* (Fall 2000), "Schoolgirl's Crush"; *Prairie Schooner* (Spring 2003), "The Bad Secret," "A Snapshot of My Sister and Me, My First Birthday, 1957"; *Southern Review* (Autumn 2003), "My Mother Always Slept like an Angel"; *Ontario Review* (Fall/Winter 2003/4), "Tow-Rope," "To My Twelve-Year-Old Daughter Away at Camp"; *Antioch Review* (Winter 2005), "Hatpin"; *Artful Dodge* (Fall 2005), "I tell you," "Meter Making"; *32 Poems* (Fall 2005), "January at the Nursing Home"; *Ploughshares* (Winter 2005), "Still Waltz"; *Image: A Journal of the Arts and Religion* (Spring 2006), "The Discipline of Craft, Easter Morning."

The author is indebted to the encouragement of Donald Hall, Baron Wormser, David St. John, Jeffrey Harrison, and Sylvia Rodrigue; to Robert Siegel for his support; and to Stephen Rosenblum, without whom this book might not have been written. The author would also like to thank the D.C. Commission on the Arts and Humanities.

Contents

one

The Bad Secret

In my parents' bedroom,
the hump of my father's belly
sucked in its breath.

He was a whale, and an island,
body hair like tropical palm trees,
balls carved into coconuts or shrunken heads;

his loud snore like sonogram waves
in a tight submarine.

Oh, we were deep,
shelves under. I could recite each plateau
going down as a knife,
digging into the furnace of the earth,
that golden seed inside the heart of the planet,

where the dead go when they are no longer bodies,
where the dead go when they have just had enough.

Tow-Rope

Because I could not climb rope
in gym class,
because I had no biceps in my arms,
and gravity keeps a fat girl from trying,
because the night was rising like dough,

where my mother had fastened pink
ruffled curtains from a rod,
when I was old enough to be hidden
from sight

my father decided to train me—
in the leak-puddled basement
by hanging from the rafters
a thick, weedy tow-rope the color of straw,
and reeking of oil,
having come out of a lumberjack's woodshed.
It was a *genuine* rope, something to drag boats by,
with a double knot on the bottom
to step on, like a loose rung of a ladder—

And then I would have to pull up,
twice a day, with my father whistling in the back
while I dangled like Tarzan,
teetering from branch to branch,

and I would just hold on,
with the rope chafing me raw
and my father egging me on,
like I was a prize fighter, or a dog fetching a bone.

I would just hold on,
fearing what would collapse
from above, taking my whole house down,
and my mother, upstairs, would drop, flying,
with her hands in dishrags, and my sister
with her math books would come tumbling, and still,

I couldn't make it up an inch,
the palms of my hands sweaty with prickling rope,
as I just stuck on, like bait
or a rotisserie chicken.

I just held on, the way children
grope merry-go-round poles,
the way the grackles and robins
skittle themselves to the roofs,
or the sycamores walk on their hands,
or the way ships are clipped to the waves
so they won't slip off the sides of the sea.

What little progress I made, went into my father's ledger,
like heights in a doctor's chart,
I was sunk as a bucket
trying to drag my body back up,
a mermaid in fishtail,
an exclamation mark,
as if I were there, on display,
for all the boys to taunt,
like a hanged man
wriggling on the gallows, kicking his feet

trying to be strong.

View of the North Hospital Grounds

The world walks in rubber galoshes,
it steps into puddles
it drinks up its rain.
Can you imagine what it's like to sit
all day where you are
chained to a chair—
to watch the trees go bald,
cured of their leaves?

There is a skid in the sky,
I think a cloud braking to a stop.
Mornings, in the plaster-of-paris cast of fear,
a drum roll of the heart,
I pace the prison walk of my mind
drained by my droops, in a tailored metrical suit,
pushing into waves,
brushed through history
stammering through.
Don't dream,
Don't dream of me

In the corner of my window,
there is a peeping,
a grackle has gamboled off the twigs of the tree,
I can hear it boasting
in the nothingness of air.

There is no ground deep enough to fly down to.

All night the stumps of these black trees,
soundless as God's barking;
the trees are wired,
Medusa heads plugged into the ground.
Who says we can't hear the earth's heart beating?

The elephant insects
smooched like petals—the earth whispering
to the spiders of bones,
the fingertips of God
fitting our bodies like an evening glove.

When they told me
that my cells had screwed up,
that they had gotten the wrong idea
like arctic explorers misreading their compasses,
condemned prisoners
walking the blue, blue gangplanks
right into God,
I sensed the last travelers in the woodiness
of my own bony spine
set up a tent and build a campfire.

The stars bore out from their peepholes,
the trees were implacable,
nibbled, and slouched as cadavers in the yard,
the sky, licked clean as a cat's paw,
deaf-mute with locked jaw—

bully with one black eye—

The Discipline of Craft, Easter Morning

No use going hunting for angels,
for a Christ in the tree-mops,
a Moses winding his way up the mount
into the fire of God's fresh stubble.

There is just a serious rain,
a steady crutch for the air,
colder than any April should be.

I am up to my neck in chores:
the cat needs more food,
my daughter's clutter piles up like ant hills,
I fold her little sleeves, ghost by ghost.
What melody springs from the heart so well?

These lone trees can't be dazzled by sun today,
they have such tremors like the Pope's.
Lost loons pitched into sky folds,
their crusty buds just blinking
as if to test how fierce the light is.

They sag and meander from their stems,
they bleed from transparency.
Needless or hopeless, as overused fountains,
they are my metrics, my fortitude;
plants with lemony grass spigots
that will never go dry.

Meter Making

In the late afternoon,
the greenbottle tree is
jam-packed with leaves,
its trunk spouting
like a fountain's head.

I see the quick burnish
of sparrows bedecked
with radiant source,
red-flecked bobbers
drawn to upper stories.

What sends them to my window
only to sweep them away,
deposits of another world,
pinched with a bristle?

What rights they have:
what enunciated wings?
What makes them settle again and again,
blue-husked and identical
on my neighbor's branch,
like stress on a syllable?

The Smell

It creeps back in the night
and hangs all day,
I do everything to stifle it—
stripping the beds
of the sheets,

spraying the kitchen
with aerosol masks,
but it stays scum, a wrinkle, something
that can't be rinsed away.

It is the smell of chemicals boiling
in my skin,
the smell of the kill—
older than dough
and rising in a tin.

It is the smell of the corpse
opening its house,
like a pit eating away its fruit.

It is the smell of nothing
but what's flying away from
this green, green world,
where roses wilt like candy
or pop out of my mouth.

"Oh"

This iron sky, this lute note,
the trees have undone themselves—
into a nouveau winter

the yards, pacified, benumbed
and pale pallor, the one evergreen
clogged with inescapable leaves—

The clouds thin into contours,
drift over like slow-motion smoke,
a few birds like raisins come and go,
uneventful, a dog hoarse with temerity.

What a blank slate this sky is,
I am waiting for some cue,
a word to nibble on, *Oh*

the branches have been on a binge,
the color of soot,
all covered with tattoos.

The angels make a seamless face
behind a curtain of cloud,
they tug on the coattails of heaven.

I sniff on its trail, silting through caves,
I am a dog after its bone,
sharp as light.

It was a gold thing—
a stiff underground,
a bundle
in a jar up the road,
a skeleton suit—

The earth chewed up, picked clean of morning.

The Session

Outside, the season goes on as any oiled machine,
the leaves grind themselves out
and sizzle like bacon on the grounds,
the trees are plopped and then paralyzed
like upside-down octopuses
hooked up to heaven's IVs.

They will suck on their roots,
babies with pacifiers,
the birds tied up in a singsong.

Here is the switching of the guards,
like Buckingham Palace,
the analyst's couch with its fresh head dent,
the handstitched pillow, the tissue box
offered up like a butler's canapé;

in this near hour of guillotined minutes,
of heads basketed to drum rolls,
let me tell you my dreams—

let the world as I know it,
like any ruin,
stand as it is.

To You, *Doctor Rosenblum*

after Sexton

I had not thought of the pun in your name,
but today, walking home from the session,
I notice the roses along the yards
gargling in the light of full bloom.

Such stand-outs, with their lion pouts,
puckering like they'd just sucked a lemon,
such vivid red and yellow
champagne corks pulled-up,
freshly painted on the back of heaven.
I stop now to draw one near,
to stroke its slick, velvet petals like a cat's ears,
its inner frills sewn tightly together
as if time's tucked in.

What secrets are wrapped inside
its mummy scrolls,
hieroglyphics of the heart,
soft as pocket money?
Just an hour ago, wasn't it you who asked,
"how can you be valued by others,
if you fail to value yourself?"
Oh rose-in-bloom, I think I have found
the best of God's green body.

You stand on the brink of air,
in your flushed, pink globe,
a tiny merry-go-round
coiled on a stem,
a pincushion on kite string,
and I think you are not just a rose
but a spendthrift of love,
a never-ending peel of words
a Cyclops of buds, staggering.

Let the bees whisk to your bluffs,
to the tiny gold bricks of pollen,
to your hypothetical breath,
let your layers unfold
with your bowlfuls of sleep
like a pronged sun,
and wake with your one round eye stuck open.

I tell you

I tell you, the body is its own language
and that language is hunger—
the scabrous trees
filling in edges.

The wind, unseen, blows on its harmonica.

The squirrels reach the upper boughs
tumbling, or flinching,
in the dry nerve.

What gravity pulls downward
is met by a counterforce:
the rivers of trunks knuckling up
and feeding on air—

as if they knew
every place was their right.

two

Thinking About How Babies Are Made

I remember how I got only half of the story:

Babies are made when a mother and father
go to bed,
when the lights go out,
when they pour themselves out
like teaspoons of medicine,
when the night inserts its comma.

Babies are born when the ant-like sperms walk
across the desert of cotton sheets,
as if they were exiled Jews in a diaspora.

Babies are born when somewhere on
that great hunk of the wood bed,
two shipwrecked sailors
start a cold fire by rubbing two sticks together!

A Snapshot of My Sister and Me,
My First Birthday, 1957

This is all that I have of us,
The black-and-white Polaroid,
limp and crackled and aged—

we are sitting on the microscopic grass.
Our dresses are homemade.

You are five years old, wearing barrettes,
your hair newly grown,
and you have a sailor's collar.

I am looking elsewhere.

In the background, the dark houses
with their white shingles,
and monotonous brick

have forgotten us.

You are pushing me forward.
Already the picture is disintegrating—
it is so fragile
that some of our flesh has worn off.

My Father Throws His Camera Down
the Grand Canyon, 1968

My sister's moody,
not wanting to pose anymore
with her back to the Grand Canyon,
she's afraid of those heights;
I, too, can't look without
seeming to plunge miles and miles down,
pulverizing my bones,
stopping my blood cold.

But my father demands a snapshot
with the two of us in front of the panorama
of rock and sky, the purple peaks,
as if this were heaven:
the Colorado cliffs, the great yawn
inside the earth,
one of the twelve wonders of the world,
the color of a red, sore throat.

In front of the guardrail,
he slows the shutter,
but can't get my sister back into focus,
keeps fiddling with the aperture, the lens,
people keep getting in the way,
and he gets frustrated, and yanks
the camera from its obscene leather snout and
hurls it over the landing
like a hard throw to the outfield;

I watch it gutter down, over the pine's edge,
over the pink and orange sunset,
diving into the abyss,
with its wings perpendicular to the ravine.
By now, I have broken off
from the rest, pretending I'm an orphan—
my eyes fixed on the unseeable destruction

of my ghost in that suicidal machine.
"Hush," I say, as if hatred was a sound,
as if I could make the negative positive,
but nature itself has given up on the picture
of my happy family,
and pretends not to look
at the box with the rolled-up Kodak film
tumbling over the ledge
gathering more weight and velocity.

By now, I have lost sight of it,
shrunken to the fuzziest gauze,
blown out in one incendiary moment,
suddenly extinct,
the sum of our bodies destroyed
the minute we are exposed to light, our radiated souls
expelled like Adam and Eve's

galloping out of the garden
naked as the day they were born,
just as my father, like the strange Divine,
confounds himself with the true irony of rage,
sitting alone on a petrified stone,
knowing he's lost his only children.

Brownie Troop

We are off to do good deeds,
to baste a checkered tablecloth
or collect pennies for UNICEF,
going in a long train to Sharon Leak's house
with our brown socks,
greased leather shoes, and iron-on badges
one for merit, one for generosity—

and I am singing a ballad
about walking out on the streets of Laredo
spying a young cowboy all wrapped in white linen
and I am hearing the sins he accounts for:
gin drinking and card playing
that have left him shot in the breast and dying today,

and as I sing, I step off the curb,
sidelong into the grass thinking, this is my burden
before the coffin will seal him,
to take him to the green valley and lay the sod over him,
and I see him slumbering now,
as a bluff on the horizon,
and I know I am the messenger, playing the fife,
carrying the clumps of white roses
to cover these clods as they fall.

And, as I keep humming the lyric,
I round the corner
following my fat and thin troop
into a small tin-roofed house
where Sharon's mother
is steaming yams and wiping her brow;
and I still hear the boy in potboil smoke
rising up in ghostly wafts
and sweet stucco walls of this imaginary town I call *Loredo,*

Loredo, where the dead rise again,
between memory and grief,
where a body writhes
into lilac curtains and stubbles of blackbirds
and through the window, the tall hydrangeas
and blue washrag of sky, peeking in;

Loredo, where I am seeing the leader
in her ivory skin and delicate veins,
standing on the piano bench, conducting us
on how to write sympathy cards,
where I am seeing stale carpet stains
that remind me of blood,
and it is then that I know
that there are two songs to sing,

the one about a sad boy, condemned to the earth
and another about girlhood
and idle, interrupting dreams,
when I could banish myself there, or here,
like a cumulus cloud, or gutted wind,
or the mowed-down shade.

And I think: what world is this
that was born to sing
without a voice,
and what boy was nailed
to the open air
and bathed in rusty sunlight

and what God would let his own son die
under the outstretched palms
of a weeping willow:
here, where gusts of dandelions blow out
the early brains of their own seeds?

My Grandfather's Leg

They sawed his leg off in a cloud of ether,
but he awoke in the big hospital bed,
assuring us that he still had it.
It tingled in the way flesh meets air
in winter, and children draw a dotted line
for what will never be all the way true.

That night, above the granite roof
and peppered stars,
I imagined I saw my grandfather's leg float
back up, and twirl into space
then shuffle one step after another
and back again, until it was doing the cha-cha
just in the way he and I used to do.

High above, in its shorn pajama
the leg glided over the linoleum moon;
death, what a dance floor,
the sky's polished orchestra windy
with clarinets and flutes!

And now, years later, I expect he must have
caught up with that leg, and wrestled it back on,
so that he could keep spinning around bored
paper lanterns, embraced by the dark,
his only partner—too dizzy to stop.

Air-Conditioned House

I remember the day the fans died,
their whirlwind hearts
pried away from the windows—
dinosaurs, now extinct.
In the hourglass suburbs,
we were the first to have one:
the brick rambler
surrounded by the lake of woods,
set cock-eyed on the grass.

When the air conditioner came,
it was like a gold Buddha!
When my father lifted it out and plugged it in,
it sang like a bird, and purred like a cat.
Then, we all brought our warm pillows into the living room,
flipping them over to the cool side,
and dropped, hot and sweaty, on the carpet,
with all the windows sealed;
the air revving up its motor,
rocking the whole house to sleep.

What a miracle it was, turning the heat
into a barefoot breeze, changing the seasons.
As the cicadas shook
and darkness orchestrated our dreams,
we were bathed in this cool, sweet world of the dial,
our bodies laid out like sunburned skiffs,
lulled and washed over
in the newly invented hubbub of the sea.

To My Twelve-Year-Old Daughter Away at Camp

Already, Reveille blares over the megaphone,
you have stood at the flagpole
and eaten your stack of mulberry pancakes,
had bunk inspection,
braided your gimp into a lanyard
and dropped grape Fizzies in the bad-tasting water,
sloshed buckets of limy water into the latrines.

Today, you are a "Seneca," bunk no. 3,
sunburned and sweaty, dotted with calamine,
climbing down to the seaweedy canoes,
stinky as old sardine cans.
There is nothing I can do but pray from a distance,
there will be no sudden lightning,
or bucking quarterhorse,
that there will be no varicose vein of a root
popping up on the trail,
that the canoe always carries its orange life preservers
as you thrust those poky oars
deeper into the spongy, glass water.

Get along with the girls. Get along.
Your canoe is rocky, and dragging behind
as you keep trying the arm stroke.
I named you prematurely for strength—
a hard nut from the tree,
which is what you are, a sweet, meaty segment
of the whole. In your tight little boat
burping out of the current's beer froth.
Remember me, remember me . . .

I am your mother keeping one eye out
As you hack and chop the water with your paddles—
elbows jabbing back
like the hind legs of a shooting horsefly,
aerospace wings thrumming, and disjoining.

Hold yourself aloft:
along with the morning glories, and choking ivies
foxfire and Sweet William,
leaves so thick and curled
they look coated in black mascara.

You will be safe at arm's reach,
suctioned into the hoodlum trees
where even the owls seem spooked.
I will let you go at your own pace:
under the bridge, ducking your head,
and dodging obstacles spewing up like good spinach
you set aside on your plate.

I am your mother watching you spin out
into the squeamish current—
my point of view has grown omniscient
I can barely separate your flesh from my own,
as if we were just one river cutting into the earth,
making such slow progress along the way.

My Daughter Going to a Dance

White gloves, red satin,
sequined black skirt,
squirrel's nest, raccoon,

her lips the color of a fire-engine.
She is posing in the mirror,
with her hand tipping her hip,

whistling like a tea-kettle.

Schoolgirl's Crush

Each day, I put together more
of your life,
the way rain comes, or houses are built,
the way the rose bush sprouts
its thorns and dogged blossoms,
the way the fog holds up its yellow lantern.

What I know today that I didn't
a week ago, or a year,
I put together like a puzzle
along with the pinned-up snapshots
of a wife, and two babies,
books colliding on your shelf:

with the sound
of a light breeze at the portico,
and the blue jay's premonition of spring
and your voice that stays
through the hours

a schoolgirl's aching crush
on her first male teacher,
his face shimmering
against a blackboard's slew of grammar
drawing smoke—

such exhilarating anguish,
cupped as petals curling out
from a slender pistil into darkness
perforated by thick, frothed leaves,

and now so many years later,
as the late moon reflects back in the mirror,
I know something
more mercurial than dust,
now sweeping over the wisps of the stars,
something more stubbornly human
than I can ever touch.

Dolls' Kingdom

On a whim, it must have been—
a false alarm,
a fever gone down,
so my mother too decided to play.
She took off work
as if it were a Holy Day.

We took the bus to
Kresgee's Five and Dime,
where they had a lunch counter
in the back, next to the sewing kits,
yarn and bales of paper towels.

It was a tacky, circus place:
tangy tubs of overlit popcorn,
and blinking lanes of plastic plates,
mops, hospital shoes, a corner for pets—
like goldfish and caged gerbils,
and Hertz treats for canaries.

We sat on our swivel chairs
ordered grilled cheese
and Nehi orange soda
while the waitress wiped
down the sticky, flaked Formica,
and dealt out two paper napkins
like she was doing a magic trick.

That was the day we bought my Barbie
with a bubbletop hairdo,
in the crypt-like box,
the Barbie on Vacation
with all the accessories,
and let her go into the instant air
of cardboard living rooms.

What a miniature world it was,
of convertible walls,
closets filled with tiny high-heeled slippers
and evening wear.
We were giants peering in,
we shoved the daughter dolls
by their putty waists,
thinking up clever things to say
for each occasion,
with props replete:

the nightclub singer's plastic
authentic microphone,
or the secretary's tiny typewriter,
the model's two
drum-shaped hatboxes.
Such make-believe
ovens and patios, tennis rackets
and sequins,

all prepared for going out,
never thinking about the ends
of their lives,
or a single hour,
the heavens they'd enter,
the sentences they'd have to finish on their own,
or the delicate faces
they would have to savor
when their infinite day was done.

III three

For a Friend Who Said All Things Are Possible

for Pati Griffith

May. An early turn-around.
I steady myself
and get up from bed
to meet the morning's stare.

Fifty years ago,
someone planted the sapling
in my neighbor's yard
that rises now in a row of bark.

What I had not thought was possible
now comes flooding in,
the briny scene,
grass shining under cellophane,
the early sun
shivering like a tambourine.

And then my daughter
appears on the threshold,
overgrown hair, like Rip Van Winkle's,
awake from a hundred-year sleep.

And I touch myself at the site
of an empty womb, feel it flat again,
thinking this is what Magellan
must have felt
as he poked the wall-eyed map
and declared it round.

Negligees

From the time I was seven years old,
my mother bought me negligees,
little waspy sets, with lacy frills
sheer as snowflakes and maiden veils,
she said, would match her own.
Perhaps she'd read in some child-rearing book
that sleep could be romantic,
a little bribery in an overnight case,
which she packed up for me, along with the portable hairdryer,
and Bavarian chocolates,
so she could ship me off to Grandma's
for the Passover weekend, a grumbling woman
with a dress of somersaulting peacocks,
and ankle socks,
who smelled of must, and boiled beets,
telling me in her best English that sometimes
one can't sleep because one is *overtired*,
that groaning oxymoron, of an overlit, green-cheese moon
climbing up the fire escape of the city project,
to the 14th floor, where we watched
the Miss America pageant's talent trials—
a baton twirler, a singer, and fiddler,
blithering through the static of the agitated TV,
my grandmother painting her chewed-up nails bright red,
the color of the wobbling cherry on the ambulance
that took her away that night
with her overpumped heart palpitating,
through the stalled-up traffic of Beach Channel Drive,
with all the neighbors rubbernecking,
and me on the foldout plastic slip-covered couch,
in the drifty messianic cloud
of my Hecht's peek-a-boo negligee,
my breasts budding like an old man's flab,
the dark brambling of my nesting thighs,
standing in front of the paramedic squad,
showing what a girl can do with so much nothing.

Hatpin

My mother had many hats.
She had a white one with a brim
of daffodils, and a green felt beret
that looked smart. She had ones
with feathers and ones with veils,
like little window screens.

She told me that when she was a girl
she stuck a pearl hatpin at the back,
to use as her secret weapon
if some man rubbed up beside her on the subway
or tried to swipe her pocketbook.

I have often imagined my mother,
working on the army base
in Brooklyn in 1943,
in her mock mink and shoulder pads,
carrying a little alligator purse
in the wee hours.

Prim and always vigilant,
holding on to the overhead strap,
my mother eyed the gang of hoodlums
packing into the deserted car,
stealthily pulling out the stickpin
with iron moxy,
like a soldier uncorking his grenade.

Battleground

Stone-faced, my mother
went about her chores,
bottling herself up like vinegar.

She carried the wash out
in two huge tubs
and hung the tattered sheets and towels up to dry.

What she didn't have room for on the line
just slipped to her feet.

All day, the earth stayed stained with my father's shirts—
their hot arms twitching, and flailing
as if they still had bodies.

Falling

In the last years, my mother
couldn't keep her balance,
and kept stumbling.

They gave her a cane,
then a walker, painted her knees
with scarlet iodine,
and sent her along with a valet's bell.

Last autumn,
as we guided her under the awning
of shedding poplars,
steadying her hand, I thought

this is just how the earth
tells us one word of love,
by bringing us down to it,
so we must fall.

January at the Nursing Home

This morning, sunlight crunches the edges
of the elderly branches.
It is freezing in the yards,
the squirrels scramble to left-over grass
and the wind picks off the zeroes of leaves.

Outside the window,
I note the downed filaments
of a clawed and twisted oak,
how a few dry twigs are stuck like arrows.

In the deadlock of sky,
there is little argument.
The cold will come and go as it pleases,
it will mash up its syllables
and turn all of us inside out;

it will freeze and splinter
some indefatigable crow's wings,
and drip the ivy in caskets of ice,
thawing at last into what matters.

My Mother Always Slept like an Angel

My mother's mother taught her how to sleep,
her palms pressed together,
and clasped under her ear,
her lullaby head on the satin pillow,
her chiffon gown tied at the nape

like a barber's cape.
Oh, my mother would sleep, her dreams
tucked like those loose strands,
her widow's peak, and blonde cob.

All night, the trip of her breath
the wheeze of a see-saw,
or the tip of the scales,
upwards and downwards the heaves,
the revolving doors of a department store.

My mother dreams numbers,
a statistician's paradise of landing in evens—
she does not dream of her mother drowning in fur,
her father's stump leg,
or the plastic slipcovers in their Brooklyn apartment.

Now my mother's dementia
keeps her alert, making friends with her hallucinations,
the odd Kafkaesque machines and animals
that hover on the walls;
she can't find her way from the bed to the door;
she can't navigate her way out of her nightgown.

It takes two hours to get my mother dressed.
She is slack as a rag doll
with her sliced-off breasts.
But in the dark breath of night, she is still an angel;
she sleeps with her palms sealed,
like the good girl we send away to blessedness—

hoping she won't get lost there,
or forget her ticket number at the butcher's,
that she will remember
the first and last thing are the same,
that there is nothing to this substance of air,
but the beauty of being and not being there.

My Mother's Dementia

That is the thing about the trees—
their last wings brush upward
where they drop feathers,
the downcast lashes of an eye.

This morning my father tells me
my mother can't remember the things
she did just an hour ago,
but she can remember back twenty or thirty years—

that would make me twelve,
our house on the dry gangrene of grass,
our immovable furniture,
brass platters nailed to brick walls.

My mother was a blonde
with her hands full,
her powder compact of face cloud.

Evenings, we would watch the sun set
like a tangerine cymbal
over the nuns' residence
on grounds that bordered our fence,

the nuns tottering out
in their black habits
for evening constitutionals.
They were like blackbirds in the fields,

clutching their crucifixes,
and we looked on with a sad kind of approval
as the sun dipped under the roof of the tall weeds,
and the roses purred
in the topsoil.

We tried to regard the smallest things
as proof of their miracles,
things ruminated upon
and shelved, relics of snow,
the sloshed-up hills
and crusty boots in the shed,
the roses bustling in the afterlight.

Now, the moon rises out of memory
in a nutshell,
a stopped watch,
the black knob of night,
fastened to some celestial door—

my mother's forgetting to knock, forgetting
to ask what she came for—

In a Taxi Going Home

The driver takes the park route,
bare, black trees,
the creek's bed tattered and rocky,
the grass ruining itself.

Up on the hill, a little graveyard,
knurly headstones.
I remember now my mother's grave
is just forming a scar on the earth.

As we ride,
I find myself chasing the sight
of the cold, inner sun,
its fuzziness like the cornea of her eye.

It is too early to mourn.
Not even a month.
My mother's plain coffin is barely
cracking its shell underground.
She is only three weeks old.

Small Resurrection

When the blackbirds come,
they know their rights on earth, as if they
were halved by heaven's light.

There, on the vibrant branch,
wings tucked in, a row of little tombstones,
without a single sainted name.

What a lovely note to see them rise again
in an instant painted gold,
shaking loose this air behind them!

About Desperation

It should not be the only
form of being genuine;
there are other winds than gales,
low winds that whirl so softly

one can hardly feel.
These morning glories can't be rushed,
the engine of the bee
must be plunged deep in mazy blossom

before it sips from nectar's straw.
What else has overdone itself?
Not the sun, without a scorch;
not the blind thresh of ivy stifling the oak.

But here, at my window,
long past midnight,
I am amazed to hear the mockingbird alight
on his unseen stall,
an insomniac with a brooder's heart,
keeping such strange persistent company.

My Mother's Unveiling

After a year, they tear away
the plastic over the headstone,
baring it to the elements,
making it sting.

All day, I thought I felt my mother's hands
yanking my hair back
into a ponytail, without even a comb,
saying with bristle, and not reserve:
"Now, I can see your face!"

IV four

Wild Elms Speaking in Gold Light

When it comes to beauty,
we all have rivals.
To be consumed is something else.

A bird alights on our bronzed branches
like a torch;
it is always the same bird,
the same song,
passionately attached to the grass.

We have always been a secondary illumination,
an unrequited blaze that burns
without faith or assistance.
And you, mortals, thought it was Prometheus
who stole fire from the gods!

Still Waltz

Against an empty sky,
the elm is feathered with gold
like some apparent wing.
On the dark avenue, people pass,
lifting their collars.

Through the lit windows,
empty stairwells and still pianos.
Sparrows drive their hearts into grass.
The moon pulls aside its curtain
as if someone is peering there.
Solitude could not find a better partner.

In the winter to come,
the earth will turn its cheek,
and bear up against the cold of its own betrayals.
It is just a typical evening.
My feet burn two shadows in my path.

To an Unseen Companion

It has been this way:
the tree grows up in a difficult darkness.
By late October, half-stripped bare,
the roses sag, half-asleep.

Walking home, I pass the gardens
where the branch bristles, and snaps off,
free to travel everywhere,
as part to the whole.

It is my forty-seventh year—
along the golden paths
I think of how hard or easy it would be
to let go, now, now, in middle age, while sunlight
blurs the woods with a conspicuous flame:

Have you ever noticed that the autumn leaves
start falling from the upper berths,
as if the ones with the longest journey
float down first?

Man and Wife

I can hear the deep labor
of your breath,
where the shunt alters
the blood flow,
a spring to your heart.

We have learned to live
with obstructions,
our indurate policies,
and we have begun to keep score.

It grows so dark,
the moon quibbles
like a bubble
over the handlebar trees.

Severe oaks,
aching in their limbs,
they have gambled everything on
what will become of them:
their whole pot of leaves.

Aubade

All these places
I dreamt of you,

a man beyond middle age
turning away

in the shadows of a pond
fired by moonlight,

no longer your body,
but a force,
emerging from some thicket—

a word that stiffens
when I try to touch it,

as the bark
of a birch, or needles of pine—

as if you did not know
what hurt

the air outside you.

Middle Age

Just thinking of you,
can coax my flesh alive again,
as if that leaf could shiver air . . .

I have no body.
What has the earth to do with this?
I tense with pleasure,
like the black feelers kicking
inside the meadow lily's pinkest inner dome . . .

The downed sun kisses bark;
and the buds keep coursing through bloodstreams
of the upper boughs,
too early and too late for spring.

Watching a Ladybug on an Arm Rest at Robert Frost's House

After a quarter-turn on the arm
of the Adirondack chair,
I watch her hobble on two whisked hind legs
her tiny, scapular armor tank, topaz and metal,
her barbules like wet eyelashes,
her empyrean forewings,
leading a droll roll, blind but for the taste of light.

Hadn't I said, just a few weeks ago
that instinct is all that survives us,
now enemy or ally,
this ladybug balks and mopes along
with the same thought as mine,
wondering who will go first,
leaving it to chance, or Solomon's sword,
the sun roiling in the sand-pitted sky.

She lurches, flinching at my human gaze
and goes still again, camouflaging
herself into the ash color of the wood,
aside the lunar shadow of my hand,
as I stop to put my pen aside,
and wait, stalled, at my own border's end,
she, dug deeper in her little groove
focusing her odd little headlights,
her spotty orange and sienna fatigues.

What if one American soldier stopped
to stare the Iraqi in his eye this way,
the Syrian, the Iranian, the Palestinian, and the Jew?
What if they all ceased now,
in frozen pursuit, a poet and a ladybug,
gnashing the air after a single bone,
sharing a glimpse of the pond and its inward martyrdom

of gunning fish and mangled weed,
not wanting anything more than this—
a truce before summons,
walls that make good neighbors,
until one, not in a hurry, flies away.

Bethlehem, New Hampshire

I'd never seen the moon so large,
it was a cave with the maw
of its mouth wide open.

It was larger than a barn door
with soft hay piled inside it,
baking like a gold loaf;
a stackhouse of halos.

It was like a great bull,
flagged under the matador's cape,
it seemed to want to charge
and devour us, alive.

To a Friend Waiting for News about His Nephew's Heart Transplant

1

It is nearly spring here,
the trestles of leaves
have turned up in fresh places,
I struggle with a block,
unmotivated,

watch the saucer magnolia in my backyard
anoint its slow-motion buds,
pray for some better word to take root . . .

as a sparrow takes anchor on a bough, making it bounce,
once, maybe twice,
and the squirrel broad-jumps
from roof to roof.

2

Later, I hear that your nephew
received the heart of a 28-year-old man,
and is now at home, resting comfortably.
I write back two words:
"Thank God."

What consequences there are in the coming
and goings of any one body,
the man without a past, now
a child beginning one,
the blood circulating in its host,
the oversized heart beating
in the cramped cavity,
time fragile as the tapered fruit

of the strong-smelling flower
releasing its scarlet seeds,
dangling by threads, before shattering
its secret center on the lawn.

3
And I think of what edge of prayer
we would slice our own hopes on,
gladly, gluttonously,
wanting to breathe back the air
into the withering blossom,
back, back to when it was
just a sweet lullaby of rain,
the dark cave of the unborn
singing itself to sleep.

Bow

We learned it from the trees,
the sag down,
abject,
the weight of a laboring god
pushing the head,

marigolds,
fuchsia, and peonies—
crowning.

Making Mistakes on Purpose

Such errors there are—all afternoon:
the heater cranks to a standstill,
the telephone is off wire,
the clock is five minutes slow;
outside, the bare-bone trees
snipped out of winter, trembling with arthritis
drop snowflakes of paper.

I think of my daughter in her schoolroom,
raising her hand with an answer
and getting it wrong—
wearing an orange sweater
on a hot afternoon,
her notebook cover with doodles.
She does not think of me
although I have now entered her head
like a foot in a shoe,
the old woman in the fairy tale
who had too many children
she didn't know what to do.

There goes the wind heaving again,
leaves putter like engines running out of gas,
the gulls are airsick,
bushes are pincushions,
the triple-chinned pigeons cross
cock-eyed on the curb,
a squirrel, not knowing which way to go,
climbs up the spidery vines
of the overgrown maple and hangs by his nails,
a stuntman
defying weight and gravity.

What if we were *all* this mixed up,
what if we all didn't realize
we weren't able to fly,
but stood there, like those dull trees
flapping our arms.

Maybe God has put a spell on us.
And one day, those trees will pull up their roots
and just start walking,
like giant elephants,
heading home to the ivory boneyard,
suddenly light and reborn,
crackling their butterfly wings
and jumping like grasshoppers.

They will be an all-in-one
with their heads full of duffle feathers,
black and white spots,
snoring and meowing at the same time,
and they will march right into the ark of heaven
with their eyes still closed.

Magic Trick

Each morning, my sister
twilled the ends
of her wheat-colored braid
with a fresh rubber band.

I followed it everywhere,
as if it were a rein, a gold tassel,
a rope of silk scarves.

When I die, that braid
will be the first and last thing
I will pull
without hands.

The Clash

to Elisabeth Young-Bruehl

What a shock it was:
seeing this cardinal with wings
outspread, and jack-knifing
into the scrunched-over leaves

of the obsequious oak
making branches rock from
brusque impact,
and twigs scatter in a dither.

The gold-brained sky
surrounded it, boosting it up
until it passed like a ghost
leaving only a scarlet aftermath.

This paradoxical earth.
How it gives what it takes—
and keels at the sight of
its own clashing blood.